Productivity Through Positive Thoughts

Realise Your True Potential Through Changing Your Thought Patterns In A Positive Way

Table of Contents

Introduction

How you think defines your life.

I want to thank you and congratulate you for purchasing the book *Productivity through Positive Thoughts.*

This book contains proven steps and strategies on how to eliminate negative thoughts from your life and replace them with positivity in order to achieve a more productive life.

Negativity can affect every aspect of a person's life. It can upset health, emotions, and overall outlook on life. It can cause rifts in personal relationships and can damage one's personal reputation. Negative thoughts can cause depression, fatigue, and misery.

In this book, you will learn to assess whether you are considered a negative person and learn how to turn your thoughts around to create more positive thoughts. That is the main thrust of this text. When you have more positive thoughts in your life, everything else follows suit – happiness, good health and success.

If you find yourself feeling like "Mr. Scrooge" at the end of the day and everyone seems to avoid you, then this book will help you realize how you are making yourself miserable. If you feel like you are not accomplishing anything of value and everything you do is wrong, then you have the right book in your hands to help you turn things around.

I hope you let this book guide you in increasing your productivity by changing your negative thoughts into positive thoughts. May your thoughts increase your productivity and allow you to live a truly marvelous life.

Thanks again for purchasing this book. I hope you enjoy it!

Chapter 1 - How Negative Thoughts Affect You

If a person thinks that good things will happen, then he or she can attract positive energy and turn this positive thinking into reality. The world's best thinkers, philosophers and personal development gurus teach us that positive thinking is one of the biggest secrets to doing great things and becoming a better person. Here are some of their inspirational messages, to quote:

"Positive thinking will let you do everything better than negative thinking will." – Zig Ziglar

"In order to carry a positive action, we must develop here a positive vision." – Dalai Lama

"I have always believed, and still believe, that whatever good or bad fortune may come our way we can always give it meaning and transform it into something of value." – Siddhartha Gautama

Who are we to question or disprove these teachings, when they themselves have proven this to be true based on how they lived their lives, and look at how fulfilled and enriched their lives were. Time and time again, it has been proven that being pessimistic only brings about negative outcomes. It is like the difference between black and white or good and evil. Positive thinking brings about success while negativity only attracts failure.

But are these teachings on positivity merely based on personal experiences, theories and fabricated ideas? Do not be skeptical quite yet. There are actually a lot of studies about negativity in the field of psychology and how it can affect a person's health, mentality and success in life.

The "Negativity Effect"

One topic related to negativity being discussed in the field of psychology is the "Negativity Effect." It is a psychological phenomenon referring to the tendency of people to believe more in negative information than positive information, when it comes to evaluating the personality and behavior of a person they dislike.

There have been a number of studies done on impression formation revealing that negative information has more weight on people than positive information. A huge chunk of evidence of this is found in the field of political science. The negativity effect has been repeatedly observed on how voters process information and how it can affect the popularity of a politician.

This phenomenon states that people generally have a greater tendency to lean toward negativity. According to research, this is a common trait among young people and adults in their late years. However, it is a trait that should not be accepted as normal. This is probably the reason why there are numerous self-help books and gurus encouraging and influencing people to think positively. Negativity is innate in human nature and thus something that should be discouraged whenever possible.

The "Learned Helplessness"

Learned helplessness in psychology is a mental state in which animals' or people's minds are made to believe that they cannot control a certain situation they are exposed to, but the truth is, they actually can and are more than capable of overcoming it.

Cognitive psychologist Martin Seligman has done many clinical tests on this subject. His experiments started with giving mild electric shocks to dogs every time they tried to escape. Eventually the dogs' minds were "trained" to understand that they receive the shock when they make a move to escape, and they eventually gave up trying. The same principle was tested on human individuals but instead of using shocks, the element of noise was used in the experiment. The subjects were exposed to a certain noise and given a panel with buttons to try and "turn off" the noise. In the dog experiment, all dogs seem to adapt to the learned helplessness and gave up on the task of escaping. What was different about the human subjects was that one out of three individuals never gave up trying to find the right button in the panel to shut off the noise. What does this experiment say about humans and their ability to imbibe negative and positive traits?

These experiments give us the idea that negativity is sometimes brought about by certain aversive stimuli that we encounter in our lives that have led us to believe we are helpless to do certain tasks. When the other individuals in the experiment could not find the right button to turn off the noise they just gave up. However, a select few refused to give up. When applied in real life situations, this can be likened to people who can easily pick themselves up after rejection as opposed to others who wallow into self-pity. Some people simply have a trait that enables them to see negative situations as something that is not permanent and something that they can manipulate to become favorable. These people are the ones who rise to greatness and success. These are the people who turn into our life gurus and tell us not to give up and that we can also do great things because it really is possible. This trait of greatness can be learned, as it is only a matter of perception. Yes, optimism can be learned!

Health effects

Negative thoughts can affect your health. This is because negativity makes a person worry all the time, causing stress, anxiety and panic. Too much stress in the body causes changes in hormonal levels and neurotransmitters in the brain. This imbalance can affect cardiovascular functions, digestion, the endocrine system, brain functions and immune system.

Many people are familiar with the term "Placebo Effect" in the field of medicine. This is a method of treatment where the patient is made to believe he or she is getting medication but in fact is getting "fake" medicine. The placebo effect is used in medical research to understand how patients react to new drugs despite certain conditions.

There is another medical term called "Nocebo Effect" which describes how negative health expectations can actually cause adverse health effects. When you think you are sick and expect to experience side effects, then these thoughts actually manifest into health problems.

Psychological and emotional effects

Negative thoughts are produced in the mind, and therefore, the most critical influence it can have on a person is through thoughts and emotions. It can be the root cause of depression, anxiety, irritability, frustration and anger. Cognitive researchers Aaron T. Beck and Albert Ellis have proven through their work that negative thoughts can cause depression and not the other way around, as previously believed. Women are also twice as likely to suffer from depression and, therefore, are more prone to having negative thoughts. Women tend to over think their problems and the situations then escalate.

According to the research of Martin Seligman, depression results from habits of thought. Thus, when a person is depressed, it becomes even harder to reform the mental muscles of optimism, but with cognitive therapy, the mind can be reset to become optimistic.

Effects on personal relationships

When you are in a negative state of mind, you also tend to attract negative events and possibilities. If your aura is dark, you also tend to attract the wrong people in your life. It could be an abusive spouse, a mischievous roommate, a lousy employee, or a noisy tenant. You always seem to get into arguments with your loved ones. Relationships with colleagues seem to be difficult, and being productive in the workplace is such a challenge. You also tend to block out good fortune and the flow of abundance in your life. Negative thinking emanates from within and can show in your personality. People's impression of you will not be positive. It may seem harder to get a job, mingle with groups, or even find a life partner. Being negative does not only affect health and emotions but can also be a social burden.

On a much more personal and intimate level, being a negative person can be damaging to married life. A relationship filled with negativities can lead to a lot of arguments. A married life is not easy, and there will be many obstacles that couples face from financial burdens to problems with raising a child. If two people are not meeting eye to eye with how they resolve their life conflicts, then the relationship can easily fall into regression. It is also important for children to see positivity in their parents in order for them to imbibe the attitude. Half of the attitude that children display when they grow up is adapted from what they learned within the household.

Chapter 2 - Are You Considered A Negative Person?

You might find yourself often arguing with your spouse, partner, colleagues, family member or friends and hearing them say how negative you are. When you hear this uttered in between angry outbursts in many instances, it might be time to evaluate your personality and accept that you might indeed be a negative person.

A negative person often does not see himself as being negative. In fact, they may even think that their negative thoughts are rational. Some may believe they just have the foresight to "expect the unexpected" and be ready for the worst thing that could happen. While this may be half true, it is not a healthy habit.

So how do you know if you can actually call yourself a negative person? There are several things to ask and to assess about yourself. How do you react when problems arise in the office and in your household? How do you react to sudden accidents? How do you prepare for upcoming disasters? How do you give opinions about other people and certain issues? Do the majority of the words that come out of your mouth sound negative or positive? There are many factors to look into to understand yourself and where all the negative thoughts are coming from. Your negative thoughts might have been formed due to childhood traumas, environmental influence, social influence or even a medical condition.

To check your mental state, being assessed by a psychologist is the best approach, but there are also several online personality tests that can help you affirm if you are indeed considered a negative person. However, these online tests are not medically approved and should only be used as a personal guidance in self-evaluation.

Signs of being a negative thinker

You have probably heard of the question "Is the glass half-empty or half-full?" This is one of the most widely used tests for optimism and pessimism. Show a person a half-filled glass and ask if he thinks it is half-empty or half-full. A person who answers with half-full is regarded as an optimist, while the person who thinks it is half-empty is considered a pessimist.

This test shows that negativity is gauged by a person's perspective in life. Here are some other signs of being a negative person that might help you assess yourself.

You resist change. You tend to criticize yourself and others for failing in attempts to be perfect. You shoot down any attempts to innovate and think that things are better left off as is.

See only the bad in others. You tend to see only the bad aspect in people – how funny they dress, how they smell, how they talk, etc. You pay little attention to their good traits or they do not seem to interest you.

Constant whiner. Negative people have a tendency to whine and complain a lot about almost everything, from the speck of dust in the table to the bad service in the cafeteria.

Talk trash and even hurt people. Are you constantly getting into fights or hurting other people because of how you talk? You might be a negative talker, meaning the majority of the words that come out of your mouth are either negative, profanity or give off bad vibes.

Good people evade you. No, it is not how you look, but it is how you make them feel. While you cannot please everyone, it is a different story when people make a conscious effort to avoid you.

You find it easier to be negative. Some people simply find it easier to be angry all the time. Being good is an effort they are too lazy to exert. This is actually just a bad habit that needs to be broken, and more about how to do that is in the following chapters.

Lazy and still proud. Most negative thinkers are just plain lazy and may even be smug about it. They find it easier to be critical of others instead of making efforts to become more productive.

Psychocritic. A negative thinker constantly criticizes anything and everyone. You know you are with a negative person when all you ever talk about is failure of other people. They may even make it sound entertaining.

Beware of their wit. Unfortunately, there are also a lot of negative thinkers who are intelligent and witty. In some cases, it makes their negative opinions almost seem valid, but it can also get them into trouble a lot faster.

They wallow in negative feelings. Negative people wallow in self-pity and sorrow. Instead of trying to move on with their lives after an emotional turmoil such as a heartbreak or rejection, they tend to swim in their pool of melancholy. Thus, they tend to be defensive and have an "I don't care about the world" attitude.

Filled with life regrets. Negative people cannot seem to escape their past. They are filled with "what ifs" and "I wish I could have done/said this…"

"Poor me" mentality. Negative people always seem to think that they are the victim and sometimes even have an attitude of self-entitlement.

You think positive people are shallow. As mentioned earlier, most negative thinkers are actually smart, and because of this, they see positive people as shallow, naïve and easily pleased. Negative people see their cynicism and skepticism as being wise and having high standards.

Negative people do not accomplish much in life. This is because they are often unsatisfied with their jobs, have financial troubles and do not get along with colleagues.

If you find yourself guilty of having some of these traits and sincerely want a change, then it is time to let go and open up to change.

Did you know?

Having a negative trait is not completely hopeless. It is a fact that many negative people are incredibly intelligent. This is actually one reason why they always seem to be sarcastic, have a feeling of self-entitlement, and are always very critical of almost everything. In fact, some negative people are so smart that giant companies like Microsoft and Google hire them because these companies are able to turn their negative trait into something productive. These negative people are the ones who are able to see bugs in the system before anybody else. Of course, this is an exceptional case. Generally, negative people have to deal with the rest of the world, so they need to keep their negative traits at bay in order to cope with society.

Chapter 3 - Dealing With Physical Stress First

Are you ready to become a better, brighter person with a more positive personality and outlook on life? Then let's start your therapy. It is so much easier to become a positive thinker when you feel good from the inside out. Your negativity may be caused by several factors including overall health. In order to be happy and positive, one must start with being physically well first. People who live healthy lives are happier and have a better perspective in life. Being happy and healthy means generating more positive thoughts and the rest will follow. To start with, here are some tips on how to start living a happier and healthier life:

Find time to exercise.

Some might not get the logic behind making an effort to further stretch their already tired bodies by exercising. The fact is exercise releases endorphins, also known as happy hormones, which help a person instantly feel good and energized. Exercise helps release tension in tired joints and muscles. Allot just 30 minutes of exercise a day and feel the difference it makes to combat stress and uplift the spirits.

Stop eating junk foods.

Most people aim to accomplish all the tasks they need to do in a day. In between, some consume instant energy boosters such as caffeine, chocolates, junk foods, and energy drinks. These provide only a temporary energy boost, but after the effect wears off, the energy tends to immediately drop and the body feels more drained than usual. It is better to eat natural energy boosters such as bananas. Aside from it being healthy, it allows the body to sustain the energy it produces. Take time to research which foods are considered natural energy boosters. Eating right not only helps you feel good, but it also adds years of life to a body that has been damaged by stress.

Consider eating healthy.

Healthy eating means going back to the basics in regards to food preparation. This is when our ancestors did not have the convenience of buying canned or processed products. It is choosing to eat the freshest and the healthiest food options from the basic food groups. This usually means eating more fruits, vegetables, whole grains, and healthy sources of fats and proteins. This also means reducing or even completely eliminating consumption of refined grains, refined sugars, extremely salty foods, gluten, and all sources of unhealthy fats. Do not worry about having your food taste bland because there are better alternatives to salt and sugar that work just as effectively in giving flavor to food without the unhealthy effects. The healthy eating lifestyle is all about changing the way you buy, store, prepare, and eat your food, so you only get the best out of food.

See the doctor.

Hospitals can be scary, and some doctors are, too. Some people just dislike the whole process of getting an appointment, waiting in line to see a doctor who will most likely tell them something is wrong with their body, but remember that old saying, "an ounce of prevention is better than a pound of cure." Making sure your health is not causing you to constantly lose your temper all the time is very important. For instance, people in chronic pain can sometimes become very irritable and irrationally angry. They can snap at people for no apparent reason. The same goes for women with hormonal imbalances such as during pregnancy or menopause. Certain medical conditions that can alter moods include sciatica, diabetes, sleep disorders (such as sleep apnea), and psychological disorders.

Mental note!

You have probably heard all of these tips before, but most people do not actually follow them. Most of the solutions are laid out for them. All they need to do is to make a personalized health plan. There is a constant need to put emphasis on these tips because they are the most effective way to maintain good health. Remember that the aim is not to make a diet and exercise plan that only lasts a few months. The goal is to make a long-term plan to develop healthy living habits. The start of being a positive person comes from being healthy physically and psychologically. It is also important to check a person's emotional and psychological stability. If there is a cognitive medical problem involved in the matter, then all the techniques in the world to becoming positive lose their effectiveness.

Chapter 4 - Changing The Way You Talk

When you have resolved your health, the next thing you can do is to practice optimism by positive talking. This is probably the best approach to gauge your progress in just a short period of time. Changing the way you talk to yourself and to others redirects your brain toward positivity.

What does positive talk actually mean? It is a way of self-affirmation and self-encouragement. When there is a difficult task that needs to be done, tell yourself, "I can do this." When a task seems impossible, tell yourself "It's not impossible, I can find a way to turn this around."

Do you catch yourself saying these phrases to yourself and to other people?

- It's impossible.
- I can't do that.
- It's too difficult.
- I'll just finish it tomorrow.
- I'm afraid to try it.
- I'm afraid I might fail.
- I'm too tired to finish it.
- I'm not capable of doing it.
- I don't have the skills for that.

If you ever catch yourself saying these phrases, then make a conscious effort to stop yourself from talking this way and rephrase your sentence into something more productive such as:

- It's doable.

- That's easy!
- I'll try anything new at least once.
- I want to learn to do that!
- It's going to work, I just know it!
- I will do the best I can.
- I will finish it now, not later, not tomorrow.
- I am tired, but I will still do my best to accomplish it.

It may be easier said than done, but it is not an impossible task to do. Here are a few exercises you can do to practice talking positive almost all the time.

Hypnosis. Hypnotize yourself with positive words! This is not the dangling a locket in front of you and falling asleep at the snap of a finger type of hypnosis. This only means exposing yourself to more positive words and phrases. It can be done by writing down a list of positive phrases and words and reading it repeatedly. The reading part can be done in your spare time while riding the train, waiting for the waiter to bring your cup of coffee, or while waiting for the laundry machine to finish. When you see more positive words and phrases, you have a higher tendency of incorporating them into your speech. This technique works well for visual learners.

Listen to positivity. If you are more of an auditory learner, then listen to positive things instead of reading them. There are a lot of self-help audio recordings that can be purchased in stores or downloaded online to help you become a positive talker and thinker. You can also do it yourself and record your own voice giving a rundown of positive things to say. You can also try listening to relaxing music instead of lyrics that contain profanity.

Learn a new positive word every day. Become a positive talker and increase your vocabulary too! Did you know that the word "happiness" is synonymous to the words "joviality," "jollity," "merriment," and "gaiety?"

Compliment someone every day using a new positive word you learned. Did you know that there are 61 possible synonyms for the word "beautiful?" Approach a random officemate and tell her "You look so charming today. You must be having a good day!" Spreading positive words around helps you attract more positive people.

Think twice before you talk. Starting now, guard your thoughts and your mouth. Compose your thoughts before making comments and choosing your words. Talk slowly but surely.

Ask your friends and loved ones for help. If possible, tell your close friends and family members that you are currently starting your positive talk therapy. They can help by telling you when you unconsciously say something negative.

Why is it important to change a person's speech in order to become more positive? In psychology, they call this phenomenon the "Production Effect." It is a study that reveals people can remember words much better when it is said out loud rather than simply reading it silently. The reason for this is that the spoken words are now translated into speech, and it also has an auditory element that makes a person remember it better. Positive words when practiced in speech, translates into positive events.

Being a positive speaker can also help improve social skills and relationships. It is very pleasant to be around someone who always has something good to say or gives off positive vibes simply with the way they talk. These are the types of people who can become motivational speakers, gurus, teachers and great bosses. Positive talkers are able to inspire other, thus making their lives very fulfilling. Being a positive talker requires a lot of practice, but it will be very beneficial to a person's character. It can help build self-confidence and even become a factor to gaining better job opportunities.

Chapter 5 - Changing The Way You Think

Changing the way a person talks is easier than changing the way a person thinks. Negative thinking is something that may have been rooted in a person's mind since childhood. A person may have had a difficult experience during childhood that grew into a belief that life is generally difficult. A person may have grown to be 50 years old believing that life is filled with hurt, struggles and difficulties. On the other hand, a child may have undergone the same experience but approached life differently, thinking that difficulties are only temporary setbacks and happiness is something achievable. Positive thinking is all a matter of perspective.

Changing negative thought patterns can indeed be very difficult, but it is not impossible. It requires a little effort at first, a little persistence in the middle, and gentle reminders toward the end. Positive thinking is a mind exercise. Just like in physical exercises, if you want to lose fat and have six-pack abs, then you have to go on a diet and start training daily. The results cannot be seen overnight but probably after a few months. It is the same with training the mind. The results do not happen overnight, but in time, the results will be life-changing.

Here are a few tips on how to start changing the way you think right now.

Get some guidance. This book can get you started, but getting reinforcements ensures you do not falter in the future. As with all exercise programs, sometimes individuals have a tendency to hit a plateau. This means they only get excited to do the exercises for a few weeks but get tired of doing it after a few months. Then, they hit a wall, and go back to their bad habits. Getting guidance to maintain a positive mind may be from a counselor, psychologist, life coach, organization or even just a set of friends having a positive mind frame. The important thing is for them to know what you want to achieve in order for them to help you.

Be proactive. Changing the way you think is a personal fight. It is important to take control of your thoughts and actions. If you catch yourself reacting negatively to something, be quick to shift your mindset and think of something positive. For instance, when you are headed out to work and it starts to rain, instead of thinking your commute will be a hassle, think of how the rain actually benefits you. The rain makes drinking coffee so much better. Your flowerbeds back home are watered. You can finally wear your rain boots. Look for the rainbow that comes after the rain.

Learn to meditate. Learn to calm the mind and free yourself of negative thoughts. Even 15 minutes of meditation everyday can be very helpful to ease any tension in your mind that might be causing the negative thoughts. If you are completely clueless on how to meditate, taking up yoga classes is the most helpful thing you can do for yourself. Yoga can help keep your focus on your breathing instead of on your thoughts. There are also online tutorial videos on how to meditate. For some, listening to meditation music helps.

Do the 100 Days of Happiness Challenge. If you have not heard about it, this is an online campaign that encourages people to practice gratitude everyday for 100 days and see significant changes in their lives. According to Dr. Daniel Amen, an American psychiatrist and bestselling author of several self-help books, "Choose three things you are grateful for every day and within three weeks you'll notice a significant difference in your level of happiness." The idea is to think of things you are thankful for everyday and post it on your social media account such as Twitter and Facebook. You can simply keep a notebook, instead, and write the things you are thankful for everyday in that.

Positive quotes. Read them daily. A wide list of them can be found on the internet. You can even subscribe online, so you can receive daily quotes via email or through text messages. Positive quotes help inspire and motivate people to perform positive actions. It can also help beat procrastination.

The mind is trainable. If you wonder whether all this effort is going to work, do not fret because according to neuroanatomists, the brain is trainable and can be hardwired. This fact was based on the study of psychology professor Elizabeth Gould with her experiments done at Princeton University. Her research showed that brain cells can be generated at practically any age and that the brain can respond and rewire itself with certain mind exercises.

According to PsychCentral.com, there are three steps to make negative thought replacement successful.

The first is to be aware of negative thought patterns you are producing. The next is to let go of the negative thoughts, and the last step is to replace the negative thoughts with realistic positive thoughts.

STEP 1. Being aware of your negative thoughts. This simply means accepting that negative thoughts exist in you. These thoughts can be present all the time. These thoughts come up when you see something you dislike, when you feel pain, when you see a person that upsets you, or when you feel a negative emotion. Practically anything can trigger it. The thoughts come automatically in your brain, and it is very difficult to stop. This is because negative thoughts can be deeply rooted in a person's beliefs, character, and morals. When a person is diagnosed with depression, these negativities can be amplified dangerously.

The idea is to focus on your most powerful negative thoughts and dwell on them for a moment. Take time to assess where they come from. For example, you had an argument with your boss. You suddenly start thinking about so many negative things such as quitting the job, retaliating against your boss, or directing your anger toward your subordinates and making them feel your pain too. Positive people would instead act proactively and use the situation as an inspiration to do a better job to please the boss the next time. Negative people would be deeply hurt and angered by the argument, and ingrain the incident in their brains until it turns into something dark and ugly inside. When this happens, it reflects in the person's words and actions in the workplace. It hinders a person's ability to practice creative problem-solving, thus making a person unproductive.

What to do? Focus on these negative thoughts and always be aware of them. When you are actively conscious about having these negative thoughts, it becomes easier to turn them into something positive and to overcome them. Then comes the next step, which is letting them go.

STEP 2. Letting go of your negative thoughts. When the negative thought comes, it can take a lot of effort to push it out. A person can sometimes come to the conclusion that it is impossible to let the negative thought go. The thoughts seem to keep coming back and refuse to go away. The thing is, that is okay. The technique is actually not to push them out of your mind but to accept and let them go. Here is an example. With the previous argument with the boss still fresh in your mind, you come to work always hoping that the boss is not there or having a meeting somewhere so you do not have to deal with him again. You also keep thinking about writing a resignation letter and have even started browsing online for new job opportunities. You start to hate your work routine, your desk, the people you work with, and almost everything that has to do with your work. In your mind, the workplace has become a very negative place, and you do not think the job is going anywhere. This stream of negative thoughts keeps coming to you, and you cannot seem to control them. Instead of telling your brain to stop, try a different approach, and learn to relax and let go. Let the thoughts dwell in your mind for a while, but actively let them slide out. Tell your brain to let the thoughts slide away until you eventually forget about them. This is similar to an anger management approach in which you are instructed to count to ten whenever you feel the anger rising, and then take a deep breath and stay calm. When the negative thoughts come, just relax and actively let them slide out of your brain by forgetting about them and focusing on something else. You can say things like, "I hate my boss for making me do this, but at least he only made me do a report instead of making me rework the entire project." You can also tell yourself, "After this report I am going to file a vacation leave and give myself a reward." The negative thoughts may still come, even repeatedly, but the important thing is not to let them get buried in your brain. This can be done more easily when the brain is relaxed instead of constantly struggling to stop the thoughts from coming. Eventually, the brain will train itself to accept the negative thoughts and let them go, instead of clinging to them.

STEP 3. Changing your mindset. When you have practiced letting the thoughts slide out of your mind, the next step is to replace the thoughts. In order to become a positive thinker, you have to train the brain to always see the good angle in every situation, no matter how dire it may seem. The negative thoughts may still come, only this time it is not as overpowering as it used to be. It does not control your being anymore, and it does not bother you as much. This is the time you apply practices such as reading positive quotes, listening to calming music, or conjuring a positive image that triggers your positive impulses. The goal of thought replacement is actually not to completely eliminate negative thoughts from entering the mind. That is not realistic. There is no person in the world that thinks positively all the time. The only difference is how these negativities are managed by the brain.

The aim is to keep the mind from being affected by these negative thoughts and to train the brain to produce more positive thoughts instead.

Chapter 6 – How To Be A Productive Positive Person

The *"The simple act of paying positive attention to people has a great deal to do with productivity."* – Tom Peters

Even a small negative thought or action can spiral into a series of unfortunate things. Losing your temper in the morning can lead to a string of bad incidents during the day, such as losing your wallet during your commute to work, an argument with the boss or a client, spilling your coffee all over your desk, and finally getting a wrong food order on your take-out dinner. However, when you wake up feeling happy and relaxed in the morning, your entire day can be pleasant and filled with little surprises.

Positive thinking is a state of mind. Some people are naturally positive, which may be due to factors that have been ingrained in their minds since they were young. They probably grew up around positive people, in a happy family, or living a simple lifestyle. Some people tend to grow up with a lot of insecurities, sadness and depression because of the unpleasant things they experienced. For the latter, it is never too late to turn things around and become a positive thinker. Certain things just need to be done on a daily basis to train the brain to become positive.

Here are some steps you can take to help you overcome your negative thoughts and become a more productive person.

1. Listen to uplifting music. Everyone has a favorite genre of music that makes them feel nostalgic, inspired and happy. According to a 2014 article on Livestrong.com, music has the ability to modify a person's state of mind or consciousness. Music is able to make the right and left hemispheres of the brain function together instead of conflicting with each other. There have been many studies that proved music has a direct effect on a person's mood. Spend time recalling all the songs that make you feel good and collect them in one playlist. Save it on your computer, mp3 player or cell phone, so you can have easy access to it. Every time you feel a little gloomy, angry, depressed and unproductive, play some tunes and feel your mood change within just a few minutes.

Did you know that music can also help you become more productive at work? Research published on Sciencedirect.com revealed that playing background music while doing a repetitive task makes the worker more efficient. This is even with the presence of noise such as those created by machines. Other research reveals that being in a noisy workplace can halt productivity, but putting in earphones and listening to calming music can alter the situation and make work easier.

2. **Help others.** There is a certain kind of inner happiness and fulfillment that can be derived from helping others. You will never know how good the feeling is until you actually experience it. This feeling is called "Helper's High," and according to psychologists, it has something to do with the mood-boosting chemicals oxytocin and dopamine being released in the body after doing a good deed. Helping others can be done in many ways, even in

small gestures. Offer an old lady a seat on the bus, buy an extra order of your lunch and give it to a homeless person, or give your subordinates a compliment for their work. What comes around goes around, and spreading good things can reap positive things. Helping other people takes your focus away from your negative self, diverts your attention toward other things, and helps make someone's day better.

3. **Choose who you hang out with.** If you think your negativity is being amplified by the people you hang out with, consider planning something else instead of meeting up with your current companions. Talk to people who do not fill your mind with negativity but instead help you change your life perspective. Make your weekends more productive by hanging out with people with productive hobbies such as jogging, swimming and other outdoor activities.

4. **Spend time with nature.** People who spend time outdoors have a greater sense of well-being and tend to feel more alive. According to Rochester.edu, nature can help improve happiness level, increase energy and relieve exhaustion. Thus, people who spend more time outdoors are more level-headed, happy and positive. Even if you are a busy person, there are a lot of ways to spend time with nature. You can opt to eat lunch in a nearby park instead of inside a restaurant, ride a bike instead of driving, or simply start a small garden in your backyard.

5. **Grow up and take responsibility.** Negative people can have a feeling of self-entitlement, and they always seem to put the blame on others. They always play the victim, when most of the time they

are part of the problem. For instance, when the boss of a company blames the workforce for low sales, he may be overlooking the angle that his own management techniques may not be effective. Practice finding solutions to problems instead of blaming others.

6. **Get rid of things that trigger negative thoughts and lessen productivity.** This may sound a little drastic but it will surely be replaced with something more fulfilling in the long run. Do you still hold on to an item given to you by an ex? Is your gaming console keeping you indoors during free days instead of spending time outdoors and exercising? Are you getting so addicted to your social media accounts that it is affecting your productivity? If certain items seem to make you less productive and trigger bad memories and anxieties, then get rid of them. There is no point in holding onto items that prevent you from living a meaningful and fruitful life.

7. **Strive for perfection the first time around.** Always do your best in everything you do and aim for flawlessness. This saves you the stress of having to do it again or fix resulting problems. Having the mindset of a perfectionist can help you have the "never give up" kind of attitude that is a trait not found in negative people.

8. **Create a "Do not do" list.** This tip may seem a little odd, but it actually makes sense and can be very effective. Instead of the usual "To-do list," make a list of things to stop doing in order to maintain your path to positivity. These things may include things such as "Do not skip meals" (because

hunger makes your temper shorter), "Stop cursing" (because it gets negative reactions from people), "Stop obsessing about what's wrong with my nerdy roommate and instead get tips on how to be as smart as him." Make the list as personal and detailed as possible, so every time you read it the message takes a strong hold on your mind and emotions.

9. **Read a variety of self-help books.** Your journey to being positive and productive does not stop with this book. There are a lot of avenues in your life to explore in order to encourage your brain to become a positive thinker. If your negativity is rooted in depression, then there should be a conscious effort to treat the depression as well and not just focus on positive thinking. There are a variety of self-help books, instructional audio books, and motivational lectures that can help.

10. **Join a group that advocates a good cause.** There is no better way to channel those negative energies than to engage in activities that help make the world a better place. Join an organization that sparks your interest such as a religious group, an animal rights group, a motivational group, or a creative group. The members of these kinds of groups are usually positive people who want to advocate good things to make the world a better place. It is a very positive thing to be associated with these kind souls. Getting involved in the activities can help you find more meaning to life.

Productivity can be achieved automatically once the positive thought patterns are established in the brain. Positive people are always calm, inspired, more energetic and gracious. That is why they are able to achieve more things because they do not dwell on negativities and can easily move on with their lives. Positive people are actually happier and are, therefore, more productive. This is true according to the New York Times website. In a 2010 study done by James K. Harter and his colleagues, over $300 billion are lost in productivity annually simply because workers are so unhappy with their inner life that it affects their ability to be productive, creative, innovative, and committed to their work. It is important for workers to feel excited and fulfilled with their work in order to increase productivity.

Finally, how do you know you are making progresstoward becoming a more positive person? The results will be quite noticeable. You will become more approachable, and people will start talking to you and complimenting you. You will experience fewer stressful days and more laughter filled moments with family, colleagues and friends. You will feel more energized and inspired to do even simple tasks, even if it is just washing the dishes. You feel more fulfilled every time you go home from work, and daily tasks seem much easier to handle. You are also accomplishing a lot more work than usual. Your productivity level has increased and a possible promotion from work might be on the way. Life is more wonderful when lived positively.

Good luck, and may you find inner peace on your journey to becoming a more positive and productive person.

Conclusion

Thank you again for purchasing this book!

I hope this book was able to help you turn your negative thoughts into positive thoughts, but remember that cognitive therapy is a continuous process that gets easier in time. Changing the way you talk, act and think in order to become an optimist takes a lot of work at first, but it can be life-changing.

Always keep in mind that nobody is perfect. There is not one person in the world that has done everything right. Do not dwell on failures, and instead, take the lesson and move forward.

Let the tips discussed in this book serve as a guide to start being a positive person now. The next step is to apply the things you have learned in this book to your everyday life. Small efforts can lead to great things in the long run. Remember to make positivity a lifetime habit and not just a daily responsibility.

Thank you and good luck!